THE BELLE ÉPOQUE OF THE ORIENT-EXPRESS

TEXT: **M. WIESENTHAL**
ICHONOGRAPHY: **G. L'OLIVIER**

1st. Edition, January 1979
I.S.B.N.
84-7424-084-0

Library of Congress Catalog Card Number: 79-66159
All rights reserved.
This edition is published by Crescent Books, a division of
Crown Publishers, Inc.

a b c d e f g h

CRESCENT BOOKS
New York

A train traveler with his bulky baggage
A funny drawing by Daumier.

THE TRAIN OF THE BELLE EPOQUE

The Orient Express —the train of the Belle Epoque— did its last run from Paris to Istanbul in 1976. Almost a century of European history disappeared with it. Because the Orient Express, without any doubt, forms part of the political, social and economic history of the Old Continent. The creation of this line may be counted among the first attempts to make a united Europe a reality. The movies, literature and even music have contributed to the formation of its legend.

THE BELLE EPOQUE OF THE ORIENT EXPRESS

The Orient Express is not just another train. It was almost a myth. In spite of the vast changes in all fields which have characterized this century, it was the most famous train of all times. Authors, musicians, artists, and movie directors have all drawn inspiration from it for the creation of works which will appear in the history of art.

Nevertheless, the Orient Express we know today is not that luxurious train of the beginning of the century. Even the route has undergone some changes. The original route of the Orient Express passed through Vienna and Budapest to reach Istanbul. It was on this same route, close to Budapest, where Blasco Ibañez, the Spanish writer, suffered an accident.

"I get up," says the novelist. "One of my feet sinks into a soft, resilient thing wrapped up in blue cloth with golden

Inauguration of one of the first British
railway lines in 1821.

Boston was one of the First American
cities with a railway, as seen in this
1848 illustration.

British freight train, seen around Manchester in 1840.

THE TRIUMPHAL BIOGRAPHY OF THE TRAIN

The first locomotive was built in 1804 by Richard Trevethick. It was tested with great success in Wales (United Kingdom) over a distance of 14.5 kms.
The oldest railway for steam engines was the Middleton Colliery Railway, in England. The steam engines built in 1812 by Matthew Murray were used for the first time on this line.
In 1825, the engineer George Stephenson opened the Stockton and Darlington line with a locomotive he himself designed. The engine reached a speed of 24 k.p.h.
The first regular passenger line was opened on 3rd May, 1830, over a distance of 10 kilometres between Canterbury and Whitstable (Kent).
The first electrified line was opened in Berlin on 31st May, 1879, over a distance of 274 metres.

buttons. It is the belly of the waiter who was serving us a few moments before. He is lying on his back, with his arms wide open, his eyes bulging with fright and he doesn't get up off the floor, in spite of my treading on him... I can't recognize the dining car. Everything broken, everything smashed... Bodies on the floor, overturned tables, torn tablecloths, running liquid, in fact it is hard to know just which is coffee, which is liqueur and which is blood."
Blasco, so accustomed to duels and revolutions, was not too affected by this event. He got out of the wreckage as best he could, walked across the cultivated fields to the nearest town and returned to Budapest by tram. Derailments, at that time, were really almost expected anecdotes in the adventure of the journey. Expresses like the Trans-Siberian usually ran off the rails twice during the journey. The lines of the East, badly laid, showed chilling balances: over 16,000 accidents per year in a single province. Fortunately the crawling speed of the train reduced the number of victims.
As a result of political changes caused by the wars, that historic route through Budapest was replaced by a new one linking Paris with Milan, Belgrade, Sophia and Istambul through the Simplon tunnel. This train, known as the Direct Orient Express or Simplon Orient Express, the only line linking Paris and Istambul directly, remained in service until 1976.

Paris, Gare de Lyon: travellers, platforms and luggage

Several times during my life I had crossed by chance with the Orient Express in several European stations —Lausanne, Domodossola, Venice. I even remember having contemplated its furtive nocturnal run across the French countryside. The blue and yellow lights of the coaches, shining like glow-worms

London train station. Mid 19th century.

A drawing by Daumier depicting the cold suffered by third class travelers in 19th century trains.

London Universal Exhibition of 1851.
The famous Machines Hall built at
the Crystal Palace.

Inauguration of the Paris-Roven line in
1843.

Meeting of Napoleon III with Austrian
representatives in Villefranche at the
end of the 1859 armistice.

among the vineyards of Burgundy. At the front end of the train, the blue coaches of the Wagons-Lits International Co.; bringing up the tail, the cheaper class coaches ostentatiously carrying on their sides the route board, the visiting card of its long, wandering biography: Paris, Dijon, Vallorbe, Lausanne, Milan, Belgrade... To run these names off non-stop was a journey in itself, like the railway litany.

Count Leo Tolstoy died under the light of the stars in the station of Astapovo. Another great train-lover, Emile Verhaeren, one of the first poets to sing the mystery of smoke and the railway, was run over and killed by an express in Rouen station. The medical certificate sent to his widow stated the cause of death as: crushing. Neither were the Czarist bureaucrats more sensitive when they sent Tolstoy's body home in a box in the luggage van. According to the receipt signed by his widow, the package contained a corpse.

The Orient Express, when viewed from a cheap class carriage —the swine box as it was charitably known in the heroic times— was not a luxury train. In its latter days, it was the emigrants' train, bringing them up from the poor lands of the South or the Near East to the large cities of Europe. The Orient Express was the emigrants' train, the train of the medieval pilgrims of underdevelopment, the Saint James's Way for all the underfed peoples. Arabs —from Jordan, Syria, Palestine— dragged their suitcases along the stations with a Koranic resignation, with a resignation of smoke in their bitter, black eyes. The Arabs of the crude oil lands —with their chicken under their arm, the rice and mutton stew in the pot— became Arabs of the steam and the train.

When sociologists find themselves unable to defend themselves from the topics of their profession, they fall back on the statistics, more or less true or false, which explain the standard of living in different countries: telephones per inhabitant, television sets per family, tractors per acre. In reality, the best observatory to get to know a country and even a continent, is a train station platform. Europe, for

9

The London-Greenwich line, 19th century.

A change of points of the British railways of the last century.

example, contemplated from the platforms of the Gare de Lyon, from the waiting room of Zagreb station, is still a continent of smoke and emigration. The last survivors of our romantic history: the tramp with his bag, the peasant girl with her tomatoes, the gypsy with his violin, wander, lost and lyrical, sticky and lazy, along the platforms of Europe. By observing the style of their luggage, one guesses the spirit of the travellers. The "parvenu" tourists, the globetrotters of the occasion, with very few leagues under their boots, always travel with large, baroque suitcases, with the chaotic luggage of a film starlet. On the platforms of the Gare de Lyon, they basked in their elegance; at Belgrade station, where one has to throw oneself at the train like a kamikaze, they already looked like deported slaves under the weight of their voluminous baggage; at Sophia station where there is not even one charitable soul to help the traveller, the suitcase dromedaries looked pitiful. What are we to do about it! There are still folk who haven't learnt the traveller's first commandment: calculate the weight of your luggage with the idea that, sooner or later, you will have to hump it on your own back. The time has long passed when it was necessary to take a trunk when adventuring on such a long journey as the Orient Express made, a trunk just for carrying the most indispensable items: bed-linen, crockery, a couple of Holland & Holland rifles to defend oneself against the wild beasts… Edward VII never travelled from the islands to the continent —a mysterious land where the natives don't speak English— without taking his seventy

cases and trunks with him. But that was the happy era of
the bearers, the glorious era of the porters, which has gone
down in history never to return. They were the triumphal
years of the railway, when to go on holidays was a trait of
humour, the idea of an eccentric. Brigham Young, for
example, always reserved two coaches for his cortege; one
for his bishops and the other for his wives. Almost nothing
in comparison with that actress who reserved a complete
table in the dining-car for her favourite dog, which had
Viennese sliced meat for lunch.

Solemn inauguration of a French railway
line in 1860.

Plan for the first Sleeping Car made by the International Wagons-Lits Co., in 1872.

The Orient Express's most recent travellers, in keeping with the decadence of the train, went with simpler, more easily carriable luggage: a knapsack which also served as a pillow for sleeping —between Zagreb and Belgrade— on the floor in the corridor; a pouch, very useful for making friends with the tramps who got on board in Trieste or hung around the stations, and a cardboard suitcase, held together with a string, the typical luggage of the Mediterranean peoples: the necessaire that the Latin lover took with him when going on his military service.

When the trains had bathrooms

The third class traveller had no bathroom. With a little bit of luck, he could manage a ticket, for a few francs, for the

An illustration of the time: the famous Ball Mabille of Paris.

The canteen of a German train station in 1870, by K. Erwall.

public showers at Lausanne station. Here there was hot and cold water, soap. lavender, plenty of toilet paper, clean towels and even a plug for 220V electric razors. Half way through the trip, when the weather was favourable, the third class passenger took advantage of the rainwater to have a bit of a wash and brush up in the stations.

Of course the Orient Express had toilets. The job was to get to them, fighting your way through the crowd when the train was full. The job was to dig out of the toilet that fortunate mortal who had won that de luxe spot for forty winks between Zagreb and Belgrade, when the corridors were teeming with baskets, shepherds, gypsies and girls who opened the taps of their bodies and hearts —there it goes!— with a froggy smile. The truth is that the old travellers, the

The Queen's car, used by the wife of
Louis Phillipe of Orleans.

railway's heroic pioneers, didn't travel much more
comfortably either. Until 1850, there was no genius who
thought of the needs of the railway traveller. Wary folk
took their own urinals with them and the less organized,
the improvisers, took advantage of the nearest field during
a technical halt. What the eyes don't see, the heart doesn't
grieve after. Queen Victoria of England used the first
train equipped with a toilet. Until then, not even by royal
privilege, it was strictly forbidden to evacuate any urgent
need on board the train. The royal trains stopped at stations
strategically distributed by a urologist it is assumed, so that
the Queen and her ladies could give free wing to their joy.
After the invention of the toilet, the railway technology
developed like atomic energy to extravagance, to luxury.
Some compartments even had their own bath. One day, the
door of one of these cabinets was carelessly left open and
the third class passengers swooped down on it to test the
marvellous engine. The toilet comunicated directly with the
compartment of a Hungarian princess who, at that same
instant, felt the imperious need to use it. The critical situation,
the lady with her skirt pulled up, the intruders in the midst
of their ecstasy, could have been dangerous, if it had not
been for the effective intervention of the princess's
majordomo who correctly overcame the crisis by introducing,
on the spot, each of those gathered together, by his full
name: Mr. So-and-So, pleased to meet you, etc.
Worse was the misfortune of that millionairess who hired a
special van for her bathtub. At Milan the van was mistakenly
unhooked, while the train went on to Paris with her clothes
and luggage.
Yes, those were other times: the happy years of the toilet,
the era of plumbing, the century of the Industrial Revolution.
The last survivor of these luxuries today is the Blue Train,
offering its users compartments with private bath on its way
across the Republic of South Africa.

Witty illustration depicting several
aspects of a journey in the Pullman
Palace Car of the **Middland** Railway.
1874.

THE RAILWAY QUESTION — NOTES IN A PULLMAN PALACE CAR ON THE MIDLAND RAILWAY.

Emile Zola, as depicted by Manet. Zola often wrote about trains.

The Orient Express at thirty miles per hour

The traveller of the second half of the XX century now goes along with sound behind him. The traveller in the Orient Express never went so fast. It took him two and a half days to go from Paris to Istambul. From the capital of Turkey to the Italian border there was no timetable, nor time nor sound nor anything else. But these delays may now be considered to be historical. The old travellers knew that, from Vienna onwards, the Orient Express was a lost train, a train gone astray in the mysterious forever land.
At that time it hustled along from Paris to Vienna at an average speed of close on 45 miles per hour, then came hysteria, asthma, the heart attack. Roumania at 20 miles per hour. Hungary at 30. Turkey, let nobody become impatient, at any speed, God willing.
Nevertheless, the Orient Express had some famous premières. Not for nothing was it one of those trains "having

The Amazon and Olympia, two paintings by Manet, one of the best painters of the Belle Epoque.

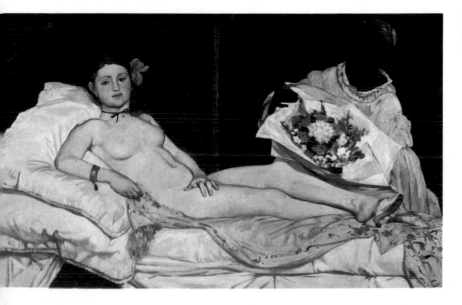

The Kaiser reviewing his troops on his birthday.

a twenty minute halt in Rouen to give passengers time to eat", as Zola commented in astonishment with respect to the first expresses.

From 1878 onwards, the fall of the Turkish Empire brought to light the importance of the Balkan markets. The countries of Western Europe urgently needed to open up quick ways of communication with the distant lands of the East. Technical progress was making the implementation of such a large work possible. The United States had given the example with the construction of a transcontinental line which reached as far as California, across the desert. The opening of this famous route, known as the Overland, was loudly feasted all across the land. Telegraph cables were even installed in church bell towers so that everyone could receive the news simultaneously, exactly to the minute and the second. The United States were also precursors in the custom of christening the great expresses with different names or nicknames, at times relating to the route and at times to a peculiar feature: The Vestibule Train (equipped with bellows connecting the coaches), the Steamboat Express (joining Boston and the neighbouring port), The Ghost Train.

Lucius Beebe wrote a chronicle of one of those heroic journeys from New York to San Francisco in five days: the engineers greased the locomotive while under way and the train came down from the mountains at the record speed of 65 m.p.h. because the airbrakes failed, of course... "With so much shaking", said the chroniclers, "it was like trying suicide to have a shave".

The inauguration of the Orient Express was no less famous. The layout of the European tracks, at least from Paris to Vienna, was much more carefully done. "In spite of the speed, one can shave", wrote the Times correspondent in his report on the inauguration. It seems that the matter of shaving was the great problem of the nineteenth century railways. Edmond About, who also went on the opening journey, provides other succulent technical details, "the magnificent refrigeration makes Normandy butter available throughout the whole journey".

Munich Central Station. Illustration by Pottner, 1881.

Working diagram of an Antée locomotive, designed by the engineer Flachat.

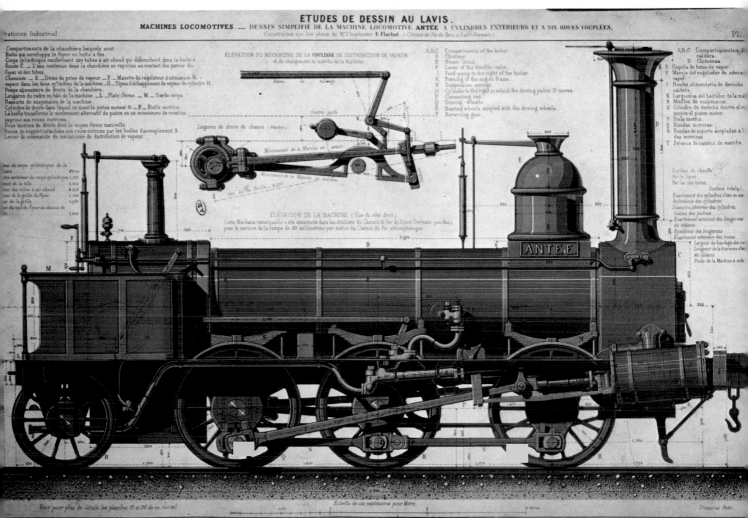

1888 portrait of the Belgian founder
of the Wagons-Lits Co., Georges
Nagelmackers, during one of his trips
to Russia.

Many obstacles had obviously been overcome for the Orient
Express to be able to start its run between the two ends of
Europe. Many Parisians crowded round the Gare de l'Est
on the 5th June, 1883, to witness the departure of the three
coaches forming the first Orient Express. The complete
journey, via Vienna, Budapest and Bucharest, took about
eighty hours. The first change was made in Giurgiu, on the
Roumanian banks of the Danube. A local train took the
travellers to the Black Sea coast; from here the travellers
reached Constantinople on board an Austrian Lloyd steamer.
The Austrian Empire, in view of its geographical situation,
was the heart of the project. But the Orient Express was
really Europe's train. Thanks to it, the Paris fashions, the
refined "esprit" of Montaigne and Voltaire reached Istambul.
To the East of Vienna, the only subject of conversation was
Europe. Everything was done in European style. Paris was
the dream of the great Ottoman lords. The corridors of the
Orient Express were adorned with the presence of those
long coated pashas who travelled with several female
prisoners; with three or four mysterious ladies which nobody,
not even the ticket collector —was allowed to contemplate.
Under the gaslights of the dining-car, the Balkan question
was discussed. The pensive afterdinner pipe could be shared
with an Indian maharaja. An English aristocrat allowed
her paleness slide over the blue velvet divans. The Express
of 1900 was a Proustian train, for exquisite, delicately
neurotic tourists.

> *Ton glissement nocturne à travers l'Europe illuminée,*
> *O train de luxe! et l'angoissante musique*
> *qui bruit le long de tes couloirs de cuir doré...*

Poets, like Valery Larbaud, wrote verses to the train. The
black cylinder of your body, the gold of your coppers, the
silver of your steel... Poets, like Walt Whitman had sung to
the train.

> *Les trains d'Europe sont à quatre temps, tandis que*
> *ceux d'Asie son à cinq ou à sept temps...*

Poets, like Blaise Cendrars, would sing to the train. On their

ORIENT EXPRESS

Route of the Orient Express from Paris to Belgrad in 1885.

Advertising poster of the inauguration of the Orient Express in 1883. This luxurious train consisted entirely of Sleeping Cars and was considered the best "cruising train" of its time.

Route and schedule of the Orient Express in 1855; the train only went as far as Belgrad.

arrival at Erzequjvar, in Hungary, the passengers were awakened by the music of czardas. It was the little homage of an old landowner of the region, who left a legacy in his will to pay for this sweet eccentricity. With another eccentricity, somewhat more boastful, Antony Bibesco, the Roumanian friend of Marcel Proust, referred to the extension of his lands:

"The Orient Express takes three hours to cross me."

But all glory, like all misfortune, comes to an end. The First World War meant the first change of points —and the first serious warning —in the happy life story of the Orient Express. With the defeat of Austria, the vital centre of European commerce was to move South. Mussolini finally won the battle and managed to divert the route, to the advantage of Italy. Thus the line of the Simplon Orient Express gradually imposed itself until our times. But the train was no longer the same paradise of luxury. Neither was Europe the same. To live in European style meant something quite different in the forties. Fascist civil servants, upstart officers, traders enriched by the black market in the First World War, Trostkyte agitators... the corridors of the Orient Express were the reflection, neither exaggerated nor toned down, but just faithful, of the new Europe.

The Orient Express, or the trains of love

The corridors of the Orient Express were the reflection of Europe: crowded in France, orderly and clean in Switzerland, noisy in Italy, packed and happy in Jugoslavia, melancholic and full of soldiers in Bulgaria, packed with parcels in Turkey... Fortunately, in the corridors of the Orient Express —that thermometre of Europe— love was also made: delicately in France, containedly in Switzerland, ostentatiously in Italy, with feeling and violins in Jugoslavia, with the permission of the authorities in Bulgaria and with secret fruition in Turkey.

Trains, with their rocking like a cradle, their agony of steam, their creak of rust and brakes, were always romantic carriages, hostels of love. Some psychologists have spoken of the erogenous power of the train. The movies have used the image of the piston as an erotic symbol.

La trepidation excitante des trains
nous glisse de désirs dans la moelle des reins.

Alphonse Allais wrote it in verse. Just as clearly as Samuel Johnson, the famous English moralist who —perhaps exceeding himself— opined that the height of pleasure was to travel alone with a lady on a shaking post-horse saddle. Apollinaire also wrote a railway orgy in "Les Onze mille Verges" which closed on a high note with a double killing in a compartment of the Orient Express. Nevertheless, the classic of the species, translated into twenty-seven languages, was published in 1925 by Maurice Dekobra:

The Madonna of the Sleeping Cars. The Madonna, as her name indicates, spent the day in bed. Every time with a different occupant. "She had received", said the author, "an exquisite sporting education in Salisbury College." The love trains were famous in England and France. Daily local trains departed from Paris and London full of young girls of sporting education, madonnas of the sleeping cars and of the slips, lyrical princesses of the railway who had discovered, like the fair people, the importance of taking the offer to the point of demand. The Free Trade ladies did their business in the first class carriages which, with curtains down, crossed London from Canon Street to Charing Cross. The journey lasted eight minutes. The business fell through when the Company, with a view to improving the service naturally, established a stop half way along the route. Five minutes travelling time. Too fast even for the most efficient executives!

The Orient Express traveled through Austrian-Hungarian lands on its way to the capital of Servia. According to this German poster the train appears to have been inaugurated on November 1, 1885.

The first Orient Express on its inaugural trip in 1883.

The Orient Express as a work of art

The love expresses have not been the only subject for railway literature. The mystery novel has drawn much inspiration from trains since Xavier de Montepin published his P.L.M. Rigole in 1860. André Gide used the movement of the train and the loneliness of the compartments in his "Les Caves de Vatican" as provocation to crime. Agatha Christie wrote one of the most classical works of this nature: The Crime on the Orient Express.

It is curious, however, that the Orient Express's mystery tradition has no real foundation. The list of crimes or violent events concerning this train is really poor. In 1891 it was involved in a kidnapping, when Macedonian partisans kidnapped four Germans and set them free on payment

of a ransom. Its chapter of intrigues is not much more
famous either. Prince Ferdinand, who wished to be crowned
King of Bulgaria, travelled from Paris to Sophia, incognito,
hidden away in a toilet of the Orient Express.
Expresses have always been a subject for literature. From
"The Human Beast" by Zola to "The Happy Death" by
Camus, From "The Traveller and Love" by Paul Morand,
to the "Orient Express" by Graham Greene. From Marcel
Proust, who considered the Bradshaw's to be "the most
intoxicating love story", to Joseph Kessel who wrote pages of
great narrative style in "Wagon Lit". Ian Fleming also has
recoursed to the Orient Express to allow his hurrying hero to
have a romantic counterpoint. James Bond and the famous
Soviet spy Tatiana meet on the Orient Express. She was the
one who was so simply dressed with just a velvet band
round her neck.
Nevertheless, since unanimity is suspicious, let us recognize
that not all authors have been train enthusiasts. Flaubert,

Two views (outside and inside) of the first Dining Car of the Orient Express in 1883.

Different menus served in the Dining Car of the Orient Express during its first trips in Europe.

TARIF

Du Restaurant du Train "EXPRESS D'ORIENT"
Der Restauration des "ORIENT EXPRESS ZUGES"

Déjeuner (Vin non compris) } fr. 4,00
Frühstück (Ohne Wein)

Diner (Vin non compris) } fr. 6,00
Dîner (Ohne Weine)

MENU

Œufs ou Poissons	Eier oder Fische
Viande chaude	Warmes Fleisch
Légumes	Gemüse
Viande froide	Kalter Aufschnitt

DESSERT

MENU

Potage	Suppe
Hors d'œuvre	Vorspeise
Poissons	Fisch
2 Plats de viande	2 Schüsseln Fleisch
Légumes	Gemüse
Entremets	Süsse Speise

DESSERT

CAFÉ, PAIN ET BEURRE............. } FR. 1,50
KAFFÉE MIT BUTTER UND BROD.

OBJETS DIVERS DE CONSOMMATION
VERSCHIEDENES

		f. c.
PAIN ORDINAIRE	BROD	» 15
BEURRE	BUTTER	» 50
CONSOMME	FLEISCHBRÜHE	» 75
ŒUFS	EIER	» 75
OMELETTE	EIERKUCHEN	1 »
BEEFSTEAK	BEEFSTEAK	1 75
COTELETTE DE MOUTON	HAMMEL COTELETT	1 75
COTELETTE DE VEAU	KALBS-COTELETT	1 75
VIANDE FROIDE	KALTER AUFSCHNITT	1 50
FOIE-GRAS	GÄNSE LEBER	2 »
POMME DE TERRE	KARTOFFELN	» 75
LEGUMES DE LA SAISON	GEMÜSE	1 »
SALADE RUSSE	RUSSISCHER SALAT	1 50
FROMAGE	KÄSE	» 50

VINS DE HONGRIE	UNGARISCHE WEINE
SUR LE PARCOURS EN	NUR AUF DER FAHRT
AUTRICHE-HONGRIE seulement	in OESTERREICH-UNGARN

KARLOWITZER	la 1/2 bouteille...... }	1 75
	1/2 flasche......	
NRZMELYER	1/2 »	1 75
TOCKAY	la	5 »

				f.
BORDEAUX 1er Choix	la 1/2 bouteille	2
Supérieur	la 1/2 flasche	3
PORTO	»	le 1/4 »	3
	»	le 1/4 »	1
SHERRY	»	la 1/2 »	3
	»	le 1/4 »	1

CHAMPAGNE

		f.
VIGNERON CARLE	la 1/4 »	5
VERZENAY IMPÉRIAL	la 1/4 »	6
	la »	12
MOËT ET CHANDON	la 1/4 »	7
	la »	13
COGNAC VIEUX (Alter)	le flacon	1
FINE CHAMPAGNE	le verre	} 1
	per glas	»
ANISETTE OU CURAÇAO		»
PALE ALE	la 1/2 bouteille	} 1
	la 1/2 flasche	
BAVIÈRE-BAYR-BIER	la	0
EAU DE SELTZ, LIMONADE, SELTERSWASSER		1
CAFÉ OU THÉ	la tasse	0

26

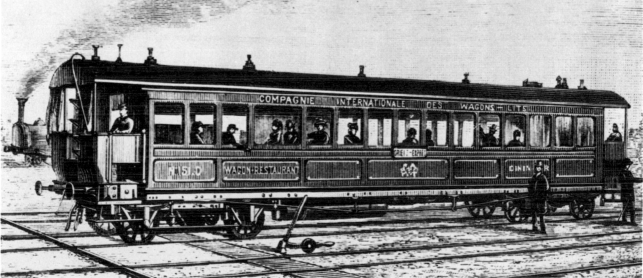

Different cars of the Orient Express in 1883: Dining Car, Sleeping Car, a bathroom and a first class wagon.

for example, cites them amongst the most sinister inventions of civilization: prisons, cream cakes, the guillotine...

And Theophile Gautier is not far behind either: "the fetid smell of coal must be included among the advantages of this way of travelling".

Right from their birth, the movies have dealt with the train. Way back in 1895 the Lumière brothers shot the arrival of a train at the station. In one of the scenes, the train is seen to move forwards right towards the spectators, causing genuine attacks of panic in the stalls. In 1924 John Ford shot "The Iron Horse", or the story of the construction of the first American transcontinental line. The Russians made the Transiberian replica in the film "Turksib". We should not forget either the comedies, above all those of Buster Keaton in "The Engineer", the story of the man who had only two loves, his locomotive and his girl friend; on the locomotive he had a snap of his girl friend and at home he had a photograph of his locomotive.

The train has been an inevitable ingredient in Westerns. And the Orient Express has also had a share in screen glory, above all in the adaptation of classical novels: From Russia with Love, The Crime on the Orient Express, etc. Paul Martin shot an adaptation of Graham Greene's "Orient Express" in England in 1934. Victor Tourjanski in Germany (1944) and Carlo Ludovico Bragaglia in Italy (1954) did the same. Artists also, from Turner to Monet, have tried their fortune

A Sleeping Car made by the Wagons·Lits International Co. and used in the Orient Express.

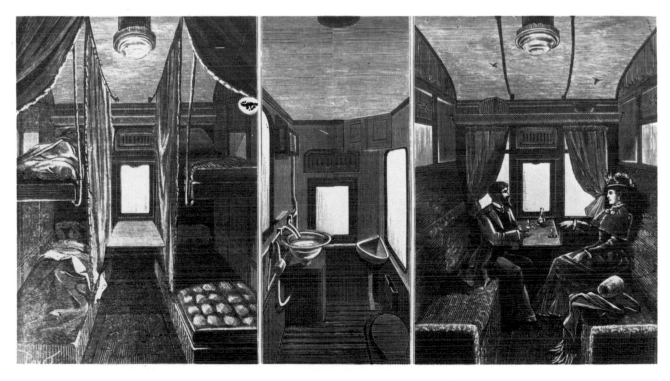

with the train. And the musical history of the expresses has composers such as Johann Strauss (Einsebahn-Lust) or Hector Berlioz who composed a "Song to the Railways". The Orient Express is, without any doubt, a train with a past.

The train has not managed to cross the sound barrier. Nevertheless, it has managed to cross the time barrier. From Paris to Istambul, the Orient Express has carried almost a century of history on its back: Paris, Dijon, Vallorbe, Lausanne, Milan, Venice, Ljubljana, Zagreb, Belgrade, Sophia, Kapikule, Istambul... The evocative litany of travel.

Europe by third class carriage: the Orient Express

The train era is fading away. It is going to just disappear one of these days and no one will notice it. The train, like 5 o'clock tea, hot broth and all the inventions that came out of the kettle, does not belong to this century. Modern day inventions are more practical and more efficient, but less human. One could feel affection to the train because it had something of a tobacco pipe, of a double-boiler about it, it reminded you of pianolas and grandfathers, fireplaces and amnions. Trains had everything but a future. They looked very much like the stew pot or like Uncle Albert's bronchitis. When the engineering of a machine bears a close resemblance to the kitchen utensils or to the weakness of the flesh, it is definitely doomed to a sad end. Good inventions, such as guaranteed vehicles, do not resemble anything else. So we are still a little bit behind the times, for the Apollo looks like fireworks rockets, and the Concorde resembles a parrot; the Volkswagen is just a bug and the Vespa scooter recalls a bidet. The engineering world gets its inspiration from the Zoo, the bathroom and kitchen utensils. We have, of course, gone far beyond the technical principle of the kettle.

During the XIX century, a whole world was based on the steam-bath, for the steam ruled everywhere: kettles, thermal

Mother and daughters: illustration of the inside of a Sleeping Car.

The Balkans were the "powder barrel" of Europe in the early 19th century, and their transgressions and political crisis motivated several wars.

Le Petit Journal

TOUS LES VENDREDIS
Le Supplément illustré
5 Centimes

SUPPLÉMENT ILLUSTRÉ
Huit pages : CINQ centimes

TOUS LES JOURS
Le Petit Journal
5 Centimes

Deuxième Année
SAMEDI 18 AVRIL 1891
Numéro 21

LES ÉVÉNEMENTS DE BULGARIE
(Assassinat de M. Beltchef en présence de M. Stambouloff)

The Imperial Car, used by Francisco Jose in 1892.

waters, "steaming broth" of the poor people and also in the poems of Ramón de Campoamor, a vapid poet, the glory of his country, but also a dirty old man who dedicated his poems to love and the express trains. Oh! for the XIX century with its steam culture and its poems sounding like locomotives:

> *Ten cannons at each side,*
> *Tracatrac, tracatrac...*
> *and with the wind-aft,*
> *tracatrac, tracatrac,*
> *full steam ahead!*

The Orient Express was already famous in 1890 as the train linking Europe and Asia: this poster illustrates how exotic a trip it was.

THE ORIENT EXPRESS IN A THIRD CLASS CARRIAGE

The author crossed Europe several times from Paris to Istambul on the Orient Express. He knew that luxury international train described in the novels of Graham Greene, Ian Fleming and Agatha Christie. But the history of the Orient Express would be tergiversated and mutilated without the portrait of its more intimate, humbler side: the third class carriage. It was in these packed carriages where the pulse of Old Europe beat, with its almost mediaeval characters: the tramp, the peddler, the gypsy musician...
In this direct, live report of the Orient Express, we have also captured the picturesque atmosphere of the stations and the impression of the cities that contemplated the passage of the most famous train of all times.

But the steam train is no longer of our times. It belongs to the past, just like the small cup of broth and 5 o'clock tea. Modern inventions are more complex, more Freudian, not so fine.
The train is finished. It still drags itself through the stations; but it already has an unmistakeable air of retired.
How great a melancholy is that of the train! What a bitter melancholy is that of these engines which are dying, like old Tolstoy, with a sheepy, vaporous look, in station sidings.

Traveling in the times of Jules Verne on a British train.

A car of the Wagons-Lits in the Niza-Vienna line, 1896.

Dramatic sketch of a derailment in France.

I am now travelling across Europe in the Orient Express. People, at the time when the train was still a luxury invention, insisted in travelling around Europe in sleeping car. Graham Greene and Agatha Christie saw the Orient Express in sleeping car. But I am crossing Europe, from Paris to Istambul, in a third class carriage. The people who travel third class have their fill of reciting rosaries with the nuns, of saying "would you like?", "No, thank you!" and "enjoy yourself", of pretending to be asleep so that the young couple in the compartment could have a little cuddle, of staring at the moon to console themselves of the cold and of the long waits on stations. Camus accused Gide of having always been a first class traveller. And a traveller who knows nothing about booking office queues, crowds pushing in corridors, the odours of the third class compartments and

Traveling for railroad engineers was not exactly a romantic trip. All romance was over for this engineer with his wife's farewell kiss.

Georges Nagelmackers in 1898: thanks to the genius of this tenacious and bright Belgian, new roads were opened for transportation and commerce.

THE ORIENT EXPRESS'S IDENTITY CARD

The first Orient Express steamed out of the Gare de l'Est, Paris, on 5th June, 1883. It covered the route via Vienna, Budapest and Bucharest to Istambul in eighty hours. When the Simplon tunnel between Switzerland and Italy was opened to traffic, the Direct Orient Express, connecting Paris directly with Istambul via Dijon, Vallorbe, Lausanne, Milan, Venice, Ljubljana, Zagreb, Belgrade, Sophia and Edirna was put into service. It covered a route of 3,070 kms in approximately 53 hours. Two branches, one from Athens and the other from Munich, linked up with the Orient Express in Jugoslavia.

the cheap station canteens, knows Europe not.
The train is dying away. It is being killed by the crisis of the kettle. But Europe, from Paris to Istambul, still smells like 5 o'clock tea and hot broth. Europe smells like smoke and a third class carriage.

A city which is already dead: Lausanne

Lausanne is a city which must have died —who knows when!— without realizing it. The world is full of cities which died in some corner of history without making too much noise. And one still likes these cities such as Lausanne, or Rapallo or Baden-Baden where people go every summer to take flowers to their past, those spas where the old folk go to die pleasantly, sweetly. There is a strange voluptuousness in that inevitable burial of memories in the mind. Some cities died with our grandparents; others with our parents and some will die —ay!— with us: But the traveller, perhaps because he has no intention of ever dying, feels a strange weakness for those characters who stroll through the cities which have already died, as if they were not aware of anything. The dustman still sweeps the streets every morning so that nobody may suspect that there is nobody living there. The flowergirl smiles at us with old, almost mechanical pleasantness, so that nobody may know that lovers no longer buy each other flowers.
The Hotel porter calls us —up-pitching his voice— Count, so that nobody may guess that no count has stayed in this hotel since 1914.
Yes, Lausanne is a city that died one day, although it hides the fact marvellously. Lausanne still performs the nostalgic pantomime of the Europe that went away. There are the monarchs who are no longer monarchs. And the unconsoled fiancees of the last Emperor of Austria. And the false sons of the Maharaja of Mysore. And Gaston Lefebvre, the last antipope who has not even managed to get himself

LE RAPIDE ET LE CHEMINEAU

Un étroit chemin accompagne en contre-bas la voie de fer. N'avez-vous jamais, le front contre la glace du wagon, suivi des yeux, avec une attention un peu puérile, de ces chemins? guetté un piéton marchant dans le même sens que votre express? imaginé d'où il venait, où il allait? Et puis la silhouette de ce passant si lent, aperçu pendant une seconde, laissé sur place, vous pourrait. Quelquefois vous la retrouvez, longtemps après, logée obstinément en votre mémoire, se détachant sur la grisaille légère du souvenir d'un ancien voyage.

Lui, le chemineau en route vers un gîte pour la nuit, ou bien le paysan qui recient des champs, rapportant au logis la mangeoire de son déjeuner, regarde d'un œil atone courir le grand rapide dans le crépuscule. Il a le temps lout juste de distinguer, dans une culture plus illuminée que les autres, des gens, assis à de petites tables, et qui mangent. Cela lui donne à réfléchir et un quart d'heure après il se grommelle à lui même : « Ils ne sont pas malins tout de même. C'est moi, si j'étais eux, qui ferais arrêter le train pour souper à mon aise, tout tranquillement, sans me faire bousculer comme ça. »

The express and the wanderer. Two ways of traveling.

The compartments of an early century Wagons-Lits car.

excommunicated.

Lausanne is a fairy tale, a garbage bin for dreams which already lost their time on the clock of history. Its villas are full of faithful, retired bricklayers who play the role of grooms. And of widows without a pension who play at being ladies-in-waiting to a princess who no longer has a kingdom or fair hair to feign it. Lausanne pretends to believe in kings, in enamoured schoolgirls, in grooms and in moonlight concerts. And perhaps for this reason it still smells of wood and linden when Europe smells of smoke and third class carriage.

The Orient Express traveller makes a halt in Lausanne. It

38

sometimes occurs to the Orient Express traveller to get down from his third class carriage to sniff a little the air which —hopeful and confused, slippery and speedy— blows through the cities. The Orient Express traveller walks along with his hands clenched around the coppers in his pockets. He stops on the wooden bridge. He pulls up in front of the antiquarian's shopwindow. He follows one woman while his thoughts are on another. And then, at nightfall, he leans back against a fountain in the Rue de l'Academie to spend a while contemplating, in the solicitude of the water and geranium, the silhouette of the Gothic Quarter of Lausanne: the iron signs, the cobbles, the cathedral spires. The Orient Express traveller writes while seated on the ground. And although he smells the linden around him, he feels nostalgia for his third class carriage. Laussanne is a city that died in one of the carriages of history. The Orient Express traveller is frightened by collective death, the death of the carriages, the anonymous death of the tracks which never come to an end. Perhaps for that reason, the Orient Express traveller likes to feel the clamour of life that sings behind him when, resting against the parapet of a fountain, he listens to the good fortune that the trickles of water sing to dead cities.

From Lausanne to Milan: the smells of Europe

From Lausanne to Milan the Orient Express traveller tries to get a bit of sleep. "Tickets please!"
At midnight the train runs along the edge of Lake Leman, speckled with lights: with red, yellow, blue lights. Night is blue in a third class carriage, like the sleeplessness of the traveller who cannot fall asleep.
"Your passport please, sir!"
Beside the traveller there is a young Norwegian fast asleep. The youth must have imaginitive, brutal dreams, soft and cruel dreams like a saga, because from time to time he shudders and cries out.

One of the famous Viennese Prater cafes, as depicted in this 1900 post card.

"Your nationality, please!", this time an Italian voice.
In Domodossola, on the Italian border, scarcely out of the fearsome gulleys of the Simplon, two Italians are fighting for a window seat. Somebody, with an umpire's vocation, proposes a Salomonic solution: half an hour each.
"Tickets, please!", Italian again.
At four in the morning, the police carry away the guy with the umpire's face who, to avoid disorders, had decided to occupy the window seat himself.
The Orient Express traveller can't sleep. But his head isn't clear either. At times he sees ghosts in the stations: first world war trains passing empty without anybody peeping out from behind the lace curtains of their windows. At times the traveller thinks that the stations also sleep and feels a strange sort of envy for the suitcases, the trunks and the trolleys abandoned on the platforms.
The traveller, neither fully awake nor fully asleep, sets about thinking of the smells of Europe. The third class carriage traveller fundamentally has a keen nose: he distinguishes countries by their smell. The sleeping car always smells of desinfectant or Eau de cologne, those heteregenous aromas which have no nationality: pale tobacco, suntan cream, white coffee. Travel guides never mention the smells of a country. Yet, nevertheless, the smells are closely related to the history and economy of people. England, for example, smells of cabbage, which is a bourgeois, conservative, monarchical and slightly neurasthenic plant. France has an old, noble, slightly stale smell: wine skin or, perhaps, simply horse urine. Switzerland smells of linden and Turkey of mutton. Countries sometimes smell of what they eat, sometimes of what they sell and there are some having no definite smell. The Orient Express traveller feels infinitely sad when thinking of those countries with no definite smell.

A romance is born: the innocent
husband reads his newspaper,
unaware of the "latest news."

An illustration of the book "Par le
Rapide," a novel by L. Halevy.

41

Milan and a waiting room

Madame Renée Nagelmackers, wife
of the founder of the Wagons-Lits
Company in 1904.

Milan, for example, so industrial, so inhabited, is one of
those cities having an unmistakeable smell of nothing
definite. The best of Milan is not the Duomo, nor the "Last
Supper" by Leonardo, but the Victor Emmanuel Gallery.
On his arrival at Milan, the Orient Express traveller goes
directly to the Cafeteria Motta for breakfast, to watch the
people passing by the Victor Emmanuel Gallery. People who
live in an industrial city have the appearance of knowing
where they are going. Perhaps because they are always going
to the same places: the office, the pub, the movies. Yes,
industrial cities smell of nothing definite like the unfortunate
flower of monotony.
Once he's had his fill of contemplating the people at the
Victor Emmanuel Gallery, the Orient Express traveller
dashes back to the station. The third class carriage traveller,
as he rolls around the world, gradually acquires some very
definite ideas on cities. Perhaps it is pride. But the third
class carriage traveller prefers the vagabond misery of the
stations to the sedentary, stale misery of the cities that smell
of nothing definite.
One, two, three, five passengers are waiting for the arrival
of the Orient Express in Milan station. Some are sleeping
stretched out on the wooden benches. An odd one is
smoking. One woman, with a white hat and lace ruff, is
knitting. The old woman has a useless, attentive gaze,
attentively useless, uselessly attentive. The sleeping travellers
are so young that most likely they have not even noticed
yet that useless look of those who await. Of what do they
think and what are they waiting for, those travellers who
wander up and down station platforms?
Europe is full of people rolling along the ways. Europe is
living through a sort of Middle Age in train, a history of
moneyless pilgrims, of wandering knights in jeans. The Orient
Express is the emigrant's train, the Middle Age of Europe,
the St. James's Way for all the underdeveloped peoples.

The travellers waiting for the Orient Express in Milan station are Indians and Arabs, gypsies and Turks. Painted in their eyes is the plaintful gaze of misery. They smell of steppe and mutton, of sandalwood and garlic. But they hope to leave Europe one day with their purse full, their shoes shining, a pair of gold teeth and fingers decorated with silver. Emigrants always come from countries where the sun shines bright. The emigrants lose the sun in the stations and mills of the cities which smell of nothing definite. And one day, they return home with clean shoes, covered with false diamonds and with false reflections of the sun in their gold teeth.

Where are the people waiting for a train at a station going? The travellers awaiting the train at Milan station must believe in Mecca or in the other life; some are smoking, others sleep. The Orient Express traveller contemplates the old woman knitting, thinks that it is not important to believe in the other life but to give life a meaning such that death and waits at stations may not snatch away. The public address system announces the arrival of a train. The Orient Express traveller always begins to philosophize at the wrong time. The public address system announces the departure of the Orient Express. And the travellers (one, two, three… five) in the waiting room stand up, stretch their legs, snatch at their suitcases with an air of reluctance and climb aboard the third class carriage. It's late now. Too late to turn back. It's eight o'clock in the morning. And as the sun rises, the Orient Express steams out of Milan, leaving behind these sad, philosophical suburbs of the industrial cities, those gone forever days where trains sleep in their sidings.

The years between 1903 and 1905 were dramatic for Europe. National minorities fought against empires. In this cover of the "Petit Journal" we see Kaiser William II during the meeting of Wiesbaden.

Italy and the railway track

Italy is still a country living open to the train. At the beginning of the century, Europe lived open to the train,

just as it lives alongside the roads today. Food, news, joy
and misfortune came by rail. Even children, who for some are
brought by the stork, for others came from Paris, as
though love felt a distant nostalgia for the rattle of the train
or the charleston.

Dad is going to Paris
in the Irun Express.
It may be for business,
or he just feels like it.

Europe and the Charleston. Children and their "buen tuntun"
(heedless ways). Our grandparents really knew what it was
all about! They really enjoyed their lives! This little rhyme:
"Dad is going to Paris... because he just feels like it", came from
an Italy that lived open to the railroad. Trains, like trams,
have something of a bachelor longing to go to Paris. If trains
are not an Italian invention (something that has not been
proved), then they should be so. Latin people invented the
"buen tuntun". Things invented by Latins are, unless God
wills otherwise, always made at random, following their
"buen tuntun".
Italy lives open to the railway track. Italy lives open to the
street. The Italians, unlike other Latin peoples such as the
Spaniards, do not fear ridicule nor are they ashamed of their
intimacy. They live in the street, they eat, they make love
and they fight in the street. The best monuments in Italy
are the washing hung out to dry and the couples necking on
the corners, the old folk dozing in the sun and the
street Arabs who, like baroque angels, calmly piss into the
public fountains.
Italy lives open to the street, rocking itself among the
washing hung out to dry on the flat roofs, basking in the sun
on the balconies, wandering along the railway tracks. Italy
laughs, with the laugh of the street urchin and tramp, of all
the illustrious monuments that history put into its heart.
From Milan to Brescia, from Brescia to Venice, the Orient
Express traveller contemplates Italy from the railway track.
On one of the walls of Verona station, a boy is chalking:
Michele fa l'ammore con la mia sorella (Michele makes love

S.M. Léopold II Roi des Belges.

H.M. Leopold II, King of Belgium,
Stanley's financial backer, colonizer
of the Congo.

Poster of a two-act musical comedy about the Orient Express as seen in a Paris theater.

"In the train". Illustration of a generation that had just discovered the exciting life aboard trains.

with my sister). Italy feels no shame. But it is absurd to feel shame when one lives open to the railway, when every day you see the faces of people passing, enclosed in a third class carriage, dragging their silence along to an unknown station.

MICHELE FA L'AMMORE CON LA MIA SORELLA: Italy is a poster written with chalk. Michele fa l'ammore... Italy is a railway. Michel fa... And the train, thinks the Orient Express traveller, whilst he recedes from Verona and the children who scribble with chalk on walls, is a machine showing how absurd distance is, how absurd are things which are left behind, effaced in oblivion: *Michele fa, Michel fa., Michele fa...*

Le grand Salon
Pera-Palace

48

Psychoanalysis of Venice

Poster of the Wagons-Lits International Co. in 1905.

The sunrise is foggy in Milan. Really foggy! Dawn is cold in Brescia. Very, very cold! The shores of the Garda lake at noon. What are the shores of the Garda lake like? They are like the wreckage of a happy day, a cloud, or like the painting of a sparrow from the hand of a homosexual or an acolyte. The Orient Express traveller wakes up in the morning with his head full of songs and riddles. The rattle on the train always brings out the poetic feelings of the traveller. If someone feels unhappy is because he wants to feel that way.

The famed Pera-Palace Hotel, on the Bosphorus. This was the hotel for the Orient Express travelers while in Istambul.

"The train and a countrywoman"
drawing by Reinhold Max Eichler.
"Jugend" Magazine, Munich.

As he goes down the steps of Venice Station, the Orient Express traveller consoles himself thinking of the people who don't feel like waking up at sunrise, of the people who have no strength to propose a song or pose a riddle to the dawn.

Along the Grand Canal of Venice, where the gondolas rock with the heavy sleep of gloved lovers or mad coffins, the Orient Express traveller thinks of the people who have already imagined, irremediably, all the riddles of the daybreak. It is sinking, it is not sinking, it is sinking, it is not sinking. Venice is a riddle, or a fortune, or a pack of cards. Venice is a vessel that does not know when its strenght will fail suddenly. It is sinking. It is not sinking. It is sinking. It is not sinking. Venice is like a question asked by man to the water or like the sinking of a biography in a well.

The Orient Express traveller strolls along the streets of Venice, posing riddles to the balconies. And to the wells. And to the canals.

What does the cloud say to the water?

The bells of St. Mark and of St. Zacharias and of St. Thomas ring out.

"What do a coffin and a gondole have in common?"

A fleet of gondolas goes down the Grand Canal. A boat sinks close to the gate of the ghetto. Children shout in the Campo Mauriziano and in the street of St. Moses and on the banks of the River St. Barnabá.

One Sleeping Car of the Wagons-Lits Co. built between 1899-1900 for the Orient Express. This car ended its days in Argel, on the Alger-Constantine line.

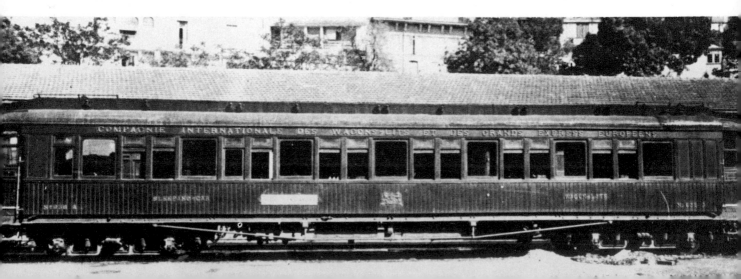

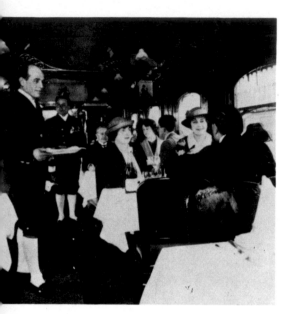

Inside a luxury train in 1912: lunch time
in the Dining Car.

"Is there anything more joyful than the washing fluttering
on the balconies over the river St. Marcuola?
There is nothing more joyful than hung-out washing. Nothing
that flies quicker than the flies across the Rialto Bazaar.
Nothing higher than the clouds decorating the campanile of
St. Mark and the church of St. Mary. Nothing wiser than the
noise of the water on the banks of the Grand Canal. No
solitude deeper than that of the whitewashed well beside
the wall or the lamp alongside the bridge.
"Really, there is nothing more joyful, nor quicker, nor higher,
nor wiser, nor deeper solitude than that of Venice in its
water."
A man and a woman wander along the Riva Schiavoni at
eventide without looking at each other. A couple of lovers
are kissing in a dead-end street. A child is playing marbles on
the parapet of a bottomless well.
Seated in the Florian Café, in St. Mark's Square, whilst the
bands churn out a repertoire learnt by heart, the Orient
Express traveller tries to contemplate Venice, ignoring the
water and refusing to be sorry for the misery of its back
streets, the loneliness of its squares invaded by flies, the
palace ruins. Venice, far from the water; at the time of its
nightfalls of white stone and yellow distemper. When the
statues disappear into the darkness. Venice, when one's
feet are tired of walking and one's eyes cannot stay open;
observed with the depth of the mind and not with the levity
of the pupils. Venice, as a psychoanalysis of man in his ruin.
The Orient Express traveller, whilst writing seated on the
terrace of the Florian Café, thinks that the best of Venice
is in the imagination. With one's back to the water and the
canals. At that time of day when one feels disposed towards
psychoanalysis or to providing a solution —yet again!— to
the riddle that the jolting of the way has placed in one's
heart.

From Venice to Lujbljana (One crosses the Jugoslav frontier and it is solemnly declared that there is no logic in the world.)

The Orient Express leaves Venice along the lagoons of Mestre, sun and salt-beds, walls and seas, stakes and grey doves. The Veneto is red and green; brick red and lemon green.
"Do you realize that there's no logic in this world?"
"Good heavens!"
The Orient Express traveller has enjoined conversation, as the train left Venice, with Dr. Alexander Wolkenstein, a Tolstoyan globetrotter who has just discovered that there is no logic in the world.
"I say, I haven't really discovered it just now."
"Oh no?"
"No, sir. On the whole, I would say that I've been harbouring

The Orient Express on the Turkish border around 1908.

6440. P. Z. - WIEN. OPERNHAUS.

the idea for more than a hundred years."
"Of course."
"One hundred and thirty two, to be more precise."
In the opinion of Dr. Alexander Wolkenstein, native of
Poltava, Province of Ukraine, there is no logic in the world.
"I say. There are two ways of looking at the world."
"With logic and without logic."
"Exactly, young fellow. I see you use your brain for thinking."
The Orient Express traveller isn't thinking anything; but he
feels his heart oppressed by dread.
"I also said that so precise a sentence almost a hundred years
ago in the novel of my friend, Leon Tolstoy, entitled Anna
Karenina. I am portrayed there under the name of Prince
Oblonski and right among my first words there's that about

A view of Istambul at the beginning
of this century: The Golden Horn port
and the New Mosque, Yeni Cami.

The Vienna Opera in a post card of the
early 1900's.

The beautiful landscape of Kahlenberg,
Austria, as enjoyed by travelers on
the Orient Express.

55

PRODIGIES OF ENGINEERING ASSOCIATED WITH THE ORIENT EXPRESS

On its run from Paris to Istambul, the Orient Express crossed the longest railway tunnel in the world, the Simplon tunnel. This tunnel was opened to traffic after four years work on 16th October, 1922, when Switzerland was connected with Italy. It is 19.8 kms long. In Vallorbe (France) the Express also went through another of the longest tunnels in Europe, the one built under the Mont d'Or, with its 6,097 metres.

The painter Josep Opisso has depicted in this charming "naive" painting a family ready to begin a journey in the Orient Express in the year of 1914.

I see you use your brain for thinking. Talented, don't you think?"

"More than talented."

"Yes, sir. When I want, I can hit the nail on the head."

The Orient Express traveller does not believe in ghosts or apparitions. But he has more than enough reasons to feel his heart in the squeeze of dread. The traveller, to hide his feelings, starts to stare out of the window. The train has just run through Monfalcone and its shipyards. On the other side of Monfalcone is the start of the upper Adriatic coastline, with its violet seas and hillsides dotted with castles.

"I say. Didn't you hear me?"

"Yes, sir. There's no logic in the world."

"That's it. And don't you want to discuss that?"

The Orient Express traveller thinks that to act deaf is a good tactic for getting rid of bores and apparitions. There are two Arabs with hostile faces in the compartment. And some tramps. And a young Jugoslav couple smoking Winston and drinking Coca-Cola. The other travellers in the compartment don't appear to take any notice of Dr. Wolkenstein. They probably think he is a Russian spy.

"I say. Have you thought how old I am?"

"One hundred and seventy three."

"Bang on. And haven't you got anything to say to that?"

"No, not particularly."

On the train's arrival at Trieste, the Orient Express traveller gets out to stretch his legs and see if he can give Dr. Wolkenstein the shake.

"Well, I warn you that I have passed the last hundred years after death. Doesn't that mean anything to you?"

The traveller, with Dr. Wolkenstein as his shadow, strolls around the streets of Trieste; the via Vicenzo Bellini, with its canal; the Vitorio Veneto square, with its fountain; the Church of St. Spiridone, with its Byzantine mosaics. While making a short prayer in the Church of St. Spiridone, the traveller hits on a new tactic to get rid of his disconcerting companion.

"Did you say you were one hundred and seventy three years old?"

"Yes, sir. And I hope to live many more yet. I say! Well I

The Orient Express crossing the last
miles of its journey on Turkish land,
in 1910.

did not believe that I had aimed so low. If I tell you that I am
five hundred years old, perhaps you won't even be surprised.
What a guy!"
"No. But what are one hundred and seventy three years?
What are a thousand years? What are a thousand million
years for the thousands of trillions of years we have to live?"
Dr. Wolkenstein stares incredulously at the traveller, with
the most astonished face anyone could ever have put on.
At times the traveller overexaggerates and makes a fool
of himself.
"Let me tell you, my dear friend, that time doesn't exist.
It is just another absurd invention of those who want to find
logic in everything."
The watermelons of Trieste are large and red.
"The idea that there is logic in the world belongs to
Aristotle who was a cretin."
The melons of Trieste have writing on their skin.
"The worst thing that one can be in this life is a classic
cretin like Aristotle, a cretin with a face like a bust."
The figs of Trieste show the red pulp of their heart through
their bursting skins.
"The whole of European culture comes from Aristotle.
And that's why it's stupid."
Trieste is the city of fruits.
"Kant was a poor fan of philosophical puzzles. But the
mistake of philosophers is to try and put the puzzles
together. Is that clear?"
"Well, rather not."

ain de luxe Milan-Paris en gare d'Iselle

The Orient Express in Austria, around 1913.

Employees of the Gare de l'Est in Paris.

The Simplon Express (1907) at the Iselle di Trasquerra station, on the Italian border.

Compagnie Internationale des Wagons-Lits
et des Grands Express européens

TENUES DES AGENTS DU SERVICE DE L'EXPLOITATION

The elegant uniforms of the
Wagons-Lits Int. Co. in 1914.

Dr. Wolkenstein stares at the sky for a moment. The he pulls his watch out of his pocket and looks at the time. Than be beats his forehead with the palm of his hand and clenches his fists.

"Because it doesn't have to be clear. Because it's a puzzle. The Devil!"

The Orient Express traveller's hunger is suddenly aroused as he strolls through Trieste market.

"Don't you think we would have a better discussion if we had something to eat?"

"Look here young man. Aristotle's idea of the unity of the world found the ground prepared in the century of the wigs.

Just note what I said, the ground prepared. Another one right on the nail, don't you think?"

The very idea of eating a watermelon makes the Orient Express traveller's mouth water.

"The XVIII century was the century of great voyages of scientific discovery. Many unknown lands were explored and the maps were drawn more or less as we know them now. And it was that, together with the pedantry of the period, which caused the theory of the unity of the world to prosper."

"I say. That's not very clear either. But one can see immediately that it is a puzzle."

Dr. Wolkenstein, the man who doesn't believe in time, pulls his watch out of his pocket again and has another look at it.

"I believe we should get back to the train. But before we do, allow me to stop for a moment to buy a watermelon."

Fashions by the designer Jean Patou around 1913. His creations were appreciated by most European belles.

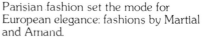

Parisian fashion set the mode for European elegance: fashions by Martial and Amand.

The renowned "Le Lapin Agile" cabaret on Montmartre, painted by Maurice Utrillo. (1910).

"Yes. A watermelon! We're going to eat a watermelon!" The Orient Express traveller has only to look at Dr. Wolkenstein's face to realize that he's been too effusive in his manifestation of approval. But the traveller is bored stiff by now with his fellow traveller's pearls of wisdom and is prepared to answer back.

"Twenty watermelons! A hundred and seventy three water melons! A watermelon for every year of your age without you having been fulminated by the blessed bolt of divine justice."

BUDAPEST. KÖZPONTI-PÁLYAUDVAR — Central-Bahnhof.

The Budapest Central Station was one stop made by the Orient Express.

Square in downtown Budapest, seen in a post card of 1910.

Budapest.

Eskü-tér. — Schwurplatz.

БЕОГРАД, Теразије
BELGRADE. La place Terazia

Terazje Square in Belgrade, with the towers of the luxurious Moskva Hotel. Below: Bucarest's Elisabeta Boulevard.

Bucuresti. Bulevardul Elisabeta.

Constantinople. *Vue de Scutari.*
Scutari.

"Calm down, young man, calm down. I see that you are not prepared to resist the concupiscence of fruit, the sinful pleasure of the watermelon. Remember that the Bible associates man's first sin with fruit."
Dr. Wolkenstein pulls up short before a fruit stall and seizes the Orient Express traveller by the arm.
"I know, my friend, that it's useless to preach to ears deaf to the counsel of experience. But before leaving, I am going to teach you a lesson that you'll never forget."
Dr. Wolkenstein opens the watermelons with the gesture of

The Usküdar (Scutari), one of the residential areas of Istambul in 1910. on the Asiatic bank of the Bosphorus.

ΛΙΘΟΓΡΑΦΙΑΙ G.A. GRISPOS PIRÉE (GRÈCE)   Η ΑΝΑΣΤΗΛΩΣΙΣ ΤΗΣ ΕΛΛΗΝΙΚΗΣ ΣΗΜΑΙΑΣ ΕΝ ΑΚΡΩΤΗΡΙΩ.   Λιθογραφείον Γ.Α. Γρυσπου εν Πειραι

Advertising poster of the famous railroad company "The Golden Arrow" which covered the London-Calais-Paris line in 1920.

Poster of the Simplon Orient Express in 1920.

Scene from the Greek-Turkish war. With the defeat of Greece began the decadence of the Ottoman empire.

DES ROSES DANS LA NUIT

ROBE DU SOIR, DE WORTH

Fashion by the noted Parisian designer Worth (1825-95). He was the first designer ever to exhibit his fashions on manikins.

a prestidigitator, as though he were going to pull a turkey out of them. Perhaps its just the traveller's hunger that's making him see all these things.

"Young man, resist the sinful temptation of fruit, diabolical symbol of the flesh and concupiscence."

Dr. Wolkenstein eats the watermelons with fruition, with authority.

"Just to show you an example, I fall into the sinful temptation of eating the watermelon."

Dr. Wolkenstein, with the fifth slice already behind him, licks his moustache, halts and then continues.

"Because it's not the watermelon that dominates me, but I dominate the watermelon."

The traveller climbs aboard the Orient Express and Dr. Wolkenstein, as the train pulls away, shouts from the platform.

"It's not the watermelon that dominates me, but I dominate the watermelon. I eat it when I want and don't eat it when I don't want."

In the third class carriage, the young Jugoslavs share out their food with enamoured, gallant generosity. The tramps divide the rancid provisions of their bags with a strict logic, with respectful, sad justice. The Arabs are sleeping off the drowsiness of their excellent lunch.

The Orient Express traveller fasts. But he is convinced that there is no logic in the world. In Villa Opicina, the first Jugoslav station, while waiting for the police to sign a visa for him, the Orient Express traveller meets up with a bearded Venezuelan who came East to try the advantages of the revolution.

"I say. Is that red beard you're sporting a symbol of your revolutionary ideology?"

The Orient Express traveller has had enough for one day.

"Look here, little man. I don't believe in the logic of the world nor in the eighteenth century explorers nor in Aristotle. I believe that the wigged century is perfect ground for anything you want. I am not thinking of ever putting the brake on my appetite. I admit that we're not going to put any jigsaw puzzle together here. And right now, although

Poster of the
Simplon Orient
Express around
1927.

I would have to punch you on the nose, I'm going to eat a watermelon to preach to you with example that it is I that dominate the watermelon and not the watermelon that dominates me."

The Venezuelan of the revolution goes as white as a sheet as though he were going to have a heart attack. The Venezuelan of the revolution has to lean against the wall so as not to die of fright. Perhaps the Venezuelan of the revolution thinks that in the world, so rotten as it is, there is not even logic.

Ljubljana, castles and hearts

Picturesque inlaid work in a car of the Orient Express.

Slovenia is innocent and green, Franciscan and sweet. The evening is opening out as the Orient Express traveller runs through the woods of Slovenia, adorned with a late spring. In Logatec, the wind whistles through the pinetrees. The river Ljubljianka flows silently and slowly through Vrinika. The Orient Express traveller, while contemplating the landscape, wonders why the colours have such an imprecise meaning. Green, according to the experts in the matter, is the colour of hope. For the medieval troubadors, it was the colour of pretence. In this respect, the traveller remembers that his forebear, Adam of Halle, troubador to the Court of France, always wore green when he wanted to hide his love for a lady; he wore white when declaring his love, wore red when he became the paladin of his lady and wore yellow garments when he could pull his plan off to perfection. Adam of Halle really had some too complicated ideas on love and spent in salvos the strength that others, in the same situation, spend on powder.

Ljubljana is innocent and green, ancient and green. Whilst strolling through the streets of Ljubljana, the Orient Express traveller thinks, that in colour question, he is not in agreement with Adam of Halle. To the traveller's eyes, green

The refined Dining Car service offered in the trains of the epoch.

is not the colour of hope, nor the colour of pretence. Green is the colour of innocence, the candorous shade of good faith, the pale moss that grows in those hearts where, who knows why, pureness still inhabits.

Yes, Ljubljana is the green city of innocence. Its streets run up the hill like the dreams of a child assembling the bricks of his castle. And the fountains of Lujubljana? The fountains sound like christening and purification, like glass and fried silver. And then the windows, looking out over a jigsaw puzzle of roofs, over an elementary architecture of tiles and bricks. A child would never have imagined a city made so to his size, so like cork and so inhabited, nevertheless by the diminute legend of Life. There is, of course, a green river reflecting the willows and the little stone bridges crossed by bicycles. And, above all, on top of the green hill, there is a stone castle, blind like the eyes of a repentant heart, covered by orange tinged clouds at nightfall. The Orient Express traveller feels innocent and green, reconciled and at peace, while he climbs the steep hill of the Ulica na Grad, leading to the castle of Ljubljana. Night is

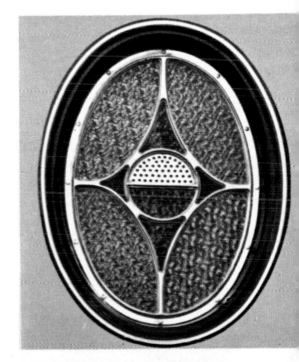

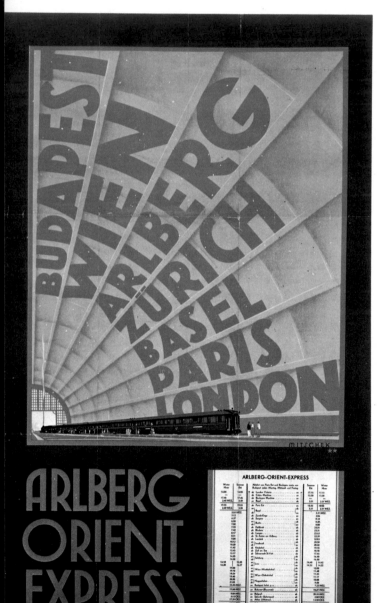

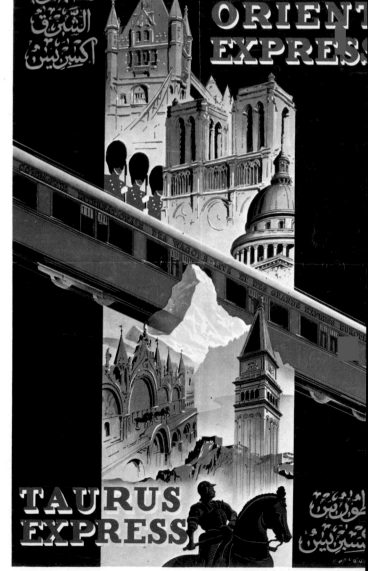

falling and the children are playing in the paths of the wood
The houses open up the shutters adorned with red hearts
to the ventilated air of the evening. Ljubljana, like Austria,
like Switzerland, like all those parts of the world having the
green of innocence, paints red hearts on its doors. Castles
and red hearts. Castles in the air, castles built of cards and
cards with hearts.
Sometimes the Orient Express traveller get involved in
transcendental philosophy. Our traveller became so
philosophic that his friends had to put to bed under a sign
that read "God is Christ." In the Kavarna bar, relaxing on a
terrace, and staring around him, the Orient Express traveller
began to feel, after many, many drinks, like a transcendental
philosopher. At the ODPRT cabaret (in Jugoslav it may mean
something), the traveller kept on with his yoga of black coffee
and striptease. When he went to bed that night he would not
be so sure that green is the colour of innocente. Even his
great-grandfather, Adam of Halle, the transcendental poet,
credited playboy and elegant troubadour, would have been
unable to say a word in this situation.

Tag for the Orient Express travelers'
luggage.

Zagreb and some ties

Dust you are and to dust you will return. It's obvious, since
it's in the Bible, that man was made from dust. Many towns,
like London or Paris or Istambul were born beside the sea
and rivers. Perhaps they are not dust but water or a
shipwreck at sea.

> "Our lives are rivers
> that run to the sea.
> That's when we die."

Whilst wandering along the streets of Zagreb, the traveller
happens to think about death: the streets are cold, purple,
deserted like the dark beat of pained, drowned soul.

Poster of the route of the Arlberg Orient
Express. To the right another poster
announcing the Simplon Orient Express
and the Taurus Express, in 1929.

The Orient Express obstructed by the snow. A novel by Agatha Christie takes place in a similar situation.

There are cities which might never have existed, cities which have no reason, either good or bad, obliging them to exist. While strolling along the streets of Zagreb, geometrical and with small gardens, laid out with the strategy of Municipal police, the Orient Express traveller wonders why Zagreb exists. There are cities which grew under the protection of a miracle, such as Bethlehem or Mecca. But Zagreb has no prodigy in its history, nor portents of any kind. The only thing worthy of mention in Zagreb, to the traveller's mind, is its ties. The cathedral isn't bad either; but it can't compare with the pattern and colour of the ties. The cathedral is Gothic. The ties are blue and red, striped and plain. The cathedral is not an invention of the Croats. The ties are. The Orient Express traveller goes round the upper town of Zagreb —the Jesuits' Square, the Church of St. Mark, the old palace of the *bans*— trying to understand how it is possible for history to disappear from a city without leaving any trace. There are pigeons flying over the upper town of Zagreb. In the lower portion of the town, not even automobiles drive around. In the upper town, the fountains spring out. In the lower town, not even the noise of hearts wanting to cry is heard. In the upper town, roses grow along the groves of the Strossmayer Avenue. In the lower town, in the shocking geometry of the Square of the Republic, white papers fly in the air. Nobody lives in the upper town of Zagreb. In the lower town of Zagreb, there are huddled together the pained lives that come from the dust and return to dust without ever having climbed the mountain to wonder whether life is river or is sea.

> *"Our lives are rivers*
> *that run to the sea.*
> *That's when we die."*

When noon heats up the awnings of the Gypsy market of Dolac, the traveller wonders whether cities have a memory. A newspaper vendor sings out with a dull voice, with a voice seemingly stifled by the ties of monotony, the news of the day, the prodigies of the time; a Hungarian woman who gave birth to triplets in an intercity coach, an

Shipping the mail in the cars of the
Simplon Orient Express, 1927.

Poster of the Simplon Orient Express
and the Taurus Express around 1930.

old woman run down by a train, the suicide of a homosexual in Shanghai, the elections for Secretary of the Party and the football forecasts. It is the 11th August, 1973, for anything, it might be the 11th August, 1954.

"In our opinion
past times
were always better."

In the station canteen at Zagreb, while waiting for the arrival of the Orient Express, the traveller wonders whether history may be knotted around one's neck like a tie. To continue pulling it tight then. While the traveller is steeped in his meditations, a woman, with a kerchief round her neck, is chatting at the neighbouring table with a fellow with a sharppointed nose who's got a fly on his moustache. There are also some gypsies with broken teeth and transparent blouses. And an overpowering smell of cheap meals.
A smell to put oneself a tie round one's neck and keep on pulling it tight.

A locomotive undergoing a test.

From Zagreb to Belgrade

Does a train have a sex? Is a train male or female?
Sex specialists are somewhat puzzled, they haven't got sufficiently weighty reasons to determine wheter a train is male or famale.
"The most difficult thing is to open their legs."
"Now then!"
"When you get their legs open, there's nothing to it."
"Of course."
At Zagreb station, the Orient Express traveller has got into conversation with Hokaido Hideyoshi, a specialized sex specialist from Osaka, who is waiting for the train to Vienna,

while sewing his pearls of wisdom among his audience.
"Yes, sir. There's no hare that gets away from me nor rabbit
that resists me."
"Of course."
"Why do you say *of course*, if you know nothing of my arts?"
"Because I see things clearly. Can't I say that?"
"No, sir. Nothing is seen clearly until you get their legs open.
Do you get me?"
To avoid a row, the Orient Express traveller steps aside and
continues immersed in his thoughts alone. Because of its
smoke, the train must be male. But it's got a female's face.
Of an old sickly female, but it's a female's face after all.
"I say. Are you going to Vienna?"
"No, sir. I'm going to Belgrade."
"Well, last month, I had to sex over thirty thousand chicks
in Belgrade."
"Well then."
"And hares. Do you know how one sexes a hare?"
"You open its legs."
"Go on. And how do you know that?"
The Orient Express traveller breathes deeply when back
again in his third class carriage, far from the refined arts of
Hokaido Hideyoshi. The train, at first sight, without going
deeper into the matter, looks female. But, perhaps, as it wears
black, it is a nun's sex.
From Zagreb to Belgrade, the Orient Express traveller sleeps
as best he can, on the floor of the third class carriage. From
Zagreb to Belgrade, there's no way of finding a free seat.
"Not even with a recommendation?"
"No, sir. This is a Communist country."
Well, there you are. Since Jugoslavia is a Communist
country, the traveller, who although not a proletarian is
travelling as a proletarian, has to sleep on the floor.
"And any complaints, to the Station Master."
Well there you are. From Zagreb to Belgrade, the Orient
Express traveller spends a bitter night, without a wink of
sleep, surrounded by a bucolic chorus of shepherds travelling
to the market in the capital to sell their chickens.
"The hardest thing is to get their legs open."

Inside of a Dining Car for forty-two
people.

RAILWAY RECORDS

Speed km/h	Type	Line	Date
46,8	Rocket	Liverpool-Manchester (G.B.)	1829
91,3	Grand Junction Railway	Madeley (G.B.)	1839
125,5	Great Western Railway	Wooton Bassett (G.B.)	1848
158,4	Philadelphia and Reading Railway	Skillmans-Belle Mead (USAS)	1890
181	N.Y. Central and Hudson River Rly	Crittenden West (USA)	1893
193,1	Savannah, Florida and Western Railway	Screven (USA)	1901
206,6	Siemens und Halske (electric traction)	Marienfeld-Zossen (Germany)	1903
230,1	Kruckenberg (propeller)	Marienfeld-Zossen (Germany)	1931
330,8	C-C SNCF (electric)	Feature-Morcenx (France)	1955
391	Linear induction	Pueblo (Colorado, USA)	1974

Employee of the Wagons-Lits Co. at the moment of the departure of the last Orient Express.

"What do you say?"

"Nothing." I was thinking of my friend Hokaido Hideyoshi, who at this time is probably on his way to Vienna, sleeping like a little angel.

From Zagreb to Belgrade, the Orient Express traveller settles himself down as best he can in the corridor, throws a gabardine over his shoulders and stretches out on the floor between a basket of tomatoes and the scented lap of a young Balkan country-girl.

"Please open your legs and then more of us will fit in."

The Orient Express traveller, with his legs open and his eyes even wider open, watches the night pass under his nose like a hecatomb. What a hell of a night the traveller spent in his third class carriage!

"Say anything?"

"Yes, sir. I can't stand being with my legs open any more."

"Well there's still six hours to Belgrade."

In the Orient Express they throw their fag ends on the floor. But they're not worth salvaging. They've been sucked right down to the end. On the Orient Express they also throw their fruit peel on the floor.

"Say anthing?"

"No, sir. Just a foolish thought. At times one just can't stand things any more and starts harbouring foolish thoughts."

The route of the Orient Express from Paris to Istambul, including the branch lines to Munich, Vienna and Budapest.

79

The towers of Notre Dame set between the twilight and the Seine.

Three aspects of Paris, the starting point of the Orient Express accross the continent.

"Well, let's see if you stop thinking, because you're upsetting the good order of this comparment."
There you are. With your legs open and without a wink of sleep!
What a hell of a night the traveller spent stretched out on the floor of the Orient Express between Zagreb and Belgrade!
"Don't dispair, we're almost there."
As the train passes by Vinkovci, the travellers legs close.
"Open your legs, man! We're stifling!"
"I'm tired and sleepy."
"Well close your eyes!"
The traveller closes his eyes between Vinkovci and Belgrade.

And his neighbour, corridor neighbour, that is, takes,
advantage of the occasion to apply himself to a mature
country-girl like a bison on heat.
"More respect for the crew!"
"Open your legs, we're stifling."
"Pull the emergency cord! This fellow'll make us derail!"
"Say anything?"
Doubtlessly the train has a sex. Male or female. But the train,
and who doubts it, has a sex. As dawn breaks in through
the windows, the Orient Express traveller feels overcome and
too weak to protest.
"We're running into Belgrade. Belgrade! Were'nt you going
to Belgrade?"
"Yes, if we get there..."
The day, luminous, open, clear, breaks over the plains sewed
with sunflowers. The train stops in the middle of a field.
Somebody picks up guitar music on his transistor radio.
The guitar sounds of sun. The accordeon sounds of
forgetfulness. The train is about to enter Belgrade. It smells

From top to bottom, three views of
Paris: The "Pont au Change", with the
renowned Conciergerie prison, where
Marie Antoniette was imprisoned;
detail of the Alexander III Bridge and
the Seine at the Isle of the Cité.

of tea. And of corn. And the charitable freshness of the
morning is felt in the air.

Belgrade: waltzes and czardas

The Danube is still the river of that Europe which smells of
smoke and third class carriage. Because rivers, although
nobody will believe it, are the soul of the geography, the
memory and the conscience of the geography. The Rhine is
an industrial river, flowing from South to North, from bottom
to top, with an anxiety of work and will. The banks of the
Rhine are strewn with factories and castles. One would say
that its waters possess a certain Faustian alchemy
converting in power or action all that they irrigate.
The Danube, on the contrary, flows from West to East,
with the laziness of a steam train or a fan of gauze, with a
reciprocation of a dance or a violin bow. There must be
some reason, although the traveller cannot find it, for the
whole humble, sentimental history of Europe to be
concentrated on the Danube.
Before continuing along his way, the traveller makes an
attempt to forget the bitter night he spent in the train, by
having a short nap on the floor in Belgrade station. Whilst
waiting for sleep to come, the traveller observes the suitcases
which roll around, without ever a complaint, on the station
platforms; the leather suitcases of the businessmen, which
always travel first class; the wooden trunk of the recruits,
which travel free in a goods van; the suitcases, once good,
but now no longer, of the widow who is travelling to meet
with her past in one of those small towns in the region
where nothing ever happens; the shiny suitcases of the
newly-weds, who love each other on the platform with a
desperate haste; the grease-stained bag of the tramp, which
never leaves its owner, as if it were the dog of his suffering.

Venice was another stop of the Orient Express. From top to bottom: one corner of the Grand Canal; a statue of the Dogos, Palace, and the bridge that leads to the ghetto.

Whilst trying to get to sleep in a corner of Belgrade station, the Orient Express traveller wonders whether a man may be defined by his luggage. The traveller contemplates his luggage: a camel hide bag he bought in Egypt, a green suitcase bearing no illustrious sign, a travelling case, full of film reels and a few books, bearing the words "Coca-Cola. Regd. Trademark" on its sides; a flute, a camera and a violin. The traveller, when he falls asleep on Belgrade Station, feels more violin than suitcase. ¡What a joy to be able to sleep with his legs open!

Belgrade is a sunbathed, happy city. In the Terazije and Republic squares, there are people who are just passing through: Montenegrans with dark moustache, fairhaired Slovenes, Serbians with white astrakan hats, gummy-haired gypsies. On the street of the Seventh of July, where the cathedral is, in the Turkish quarter, where the Mosque of Bakrakli is hidden, in the University park, in the infinite, or almost infinite corners of the old city, Belgrade sleeps. Deeply with the spirit at peace.

At evenfall, the Orient Express traveller wends his way towards the high park of the citadel, where the recruits beseige the local girls. Belgrade has its time: sunset. And its balcony: the broken wall of the citadel leaning over the Save and the Danube. The modern city, with its skyscrapers and iron bridges is seen to the South. The sun sets to the West over the confluence of the rivers in an orange and violet coloured shipwreck. Rowing boats and steamers cross the rivers. Some gypsies are playing the flute and the accordeon. Another one is playing a violin. And the recruits and the girls, hand in hand, start to dance.

Waltzes and czardas, the Danube and the Save, violins and hands. When the moon runs out from behind the cathedral towers, the Orient Express traveller, seated on a bench in the Citadel park, meditates on the meaning of rivers.

The Danube and the Save. Waltzes and czardas. Always the same innocent, sentimental story in these lands of Eastern Europe where the Danube flows with its laziness of a steam train, of a rowing boat or gauze fan.

Bulgaria: people on the stations

From Belgrade to Nis, the train runs through soft
countryside. It is raining gently, almost with resignation.
And the cattle, half grass, half sleeping, pastures in open herd
around the white cabins.
"Are you going very far?"
"No, sir. In fact, I never travel very far."
The Orient Express traveller is talking to himself. His fellow
travellers, a gypsy who is just a pure patch, a young
Jugoslav with all the look of a hippie and an old Turkish
woman who pulls her skirt up from time to time to count
her money, don't even give him a glance.
"Are you German?"
"No, sir. I've got no nationality?"
"That's right. I had one, but I lost it in a tumult."
The old Turkish women counts her money again: she packs
the large notes close to her navel and the smaller stuff in
her groin.
"I always say it. You've got to avoid crowds."
"Well, an aunt of mine lost her morals in a crowd."
"You're exaggerating."
"No, sir. There were more than one hundred thousand,
more than four hundred thousand in the crowd. I can assure
that history never saw much a crowd together."
From Belgrade to Nis the train runs along the green banks
of the Morava. From Nis to the Bulgarian border, the track
follows along the Nisava, tranquil under the rain like an old
watercolour.

The church of San Giorgio Maggiore,
masterpiece of Palladio, in the lagoon of
Venice.

The Grand Canal of Venice seen from
the Bridge of the Academy; in the
background the domes of the Santa
Maria della Salute church.

A beautiful mural painting on the Na Grad Street, in the city of Ljubljana in Yugoslavia.

"Well you must be German."

"Psch."

"With that red beard, … You're sure to be a German!"

The Bulgarian police board the train in Dimitrogravd. Soldiers armed with machine guns patrol the stations.

"They might even make you have a haircut and a shave. They don't like hippies here, you know."

"Ah!"

"And you, please forgive me for being so sincere, have rather a suspicious look. You won't be a pope who's escaped from a monastery, will you?"

"No, sir."

"Of course! With that red beard… You're German! I'm sure you're German!"

The Bulgarian police has no complaint to make of the traveller's long hair. But they do have their say on the young Jugoslav's hanging hair. The traveller, since he has escaped from the problem with a bit of luck, prefers not to stick his neck into trouble and continues to talk to himself.

"Do you speak Italian?"

"No."

"Or Portuguese?"

"I haven't the slightest idea of Portuguese."

"You do at least manage a bit of Hungarian, don't you?"

"No."

"Don't you speak anything? With that red beard…"

Bulgaria is a country having a tinge of a nomadic air, although it tries to hide it. One would say that Bulgaria wants to flee from the sweet monotony of its landscape, from the honest misery of its towns. Strolling along the deserted streets of Sophia, adorned with an endless number of gardens, the traveller thinks that poverty, when it takes root, when it is organized, is sad like stagnant water. The popes are chanting in the Church of Saint Nedelja, illuminated by a yellow reflection of candles and glass windows. In the

Church of Svetka Petka, the devout women confess sins that they will never quite commit for lack of opportunity, or for lack of imagination; or perhaps for lack of intention. It is raining, and the trams clatter across the Lenin Square with a sound of rusty scrap. Birds are flying round the gilded cupulas of the cathedral. Bulgaria seems to be a nomad who doesn't quite set out along his way, a poor man who doesn't quite burst into tears.

From Sophia to the Turkish border, the train stops at an infinite number of stations, all alike. The Orient Express traveller, who is still talking to himself, thinks that Bulgaria is like a train track and a series of stations. All alike. Sunflower and corn. Sidings and soldiers. People on the station who never go anywhere and, perhaps, don't even know where they have come from.

"Have you ever thought of being a Bulgarian?"

"Well, no sir."

"What a pity, with that red beard..."

Minarets of Edirna

The Orient Express traveller sleeps in his third class carriage while the train covers the last few yards of the world separating it from Turkey. Obviously each country has its language; but there is also a language of the stations, a confused, universal language which is heard, at night, on station platforms. They are dry, urgent sounds, sounds like a proclamation but which do not proclaim anything.

The traveller awakes in Kapikulé station, on the Turkish border, with the impression of having slept very little. The yellow lights of the station are visible through the carriage windows. It is four o'clock in the morning by the clock

Two nice corners of Ljubljana, the capital of Slovenia, one of the stops of the Orient Express.

on the brick wall. There is a poster with large letters,
excessively large for the solitude of the moment, reading:
Kapikulé.
Kapikulé station does not belong to any town. It is a halt,
a border, a clock, two benches and a name. A name written
in excessively large letters. The traveller thinks that Kapikulé
must be like the station at Astapovo, where the globetrotter
Leo Tolstoy ran up with death. At the heart of it, all stations
look like Astapovo for the traveller who, knapsack on his
shoulder, crosses the platforms in the middle of the night.
The station master, half asleep, is standing under the clock.
At Kapikulé station door, where the name is written with
excessively large letters, perhaps so as not to be mistaken
for Astapovo, the Orient Express traveller awaits a charitable
motorist wanting to take him to Edirna. And since patience
has its prize, the traveller reaches Edirna when the moon
comes out from behind the minarets of the Selimiye Mosque.
It's five in the morning and the muezzin is chanting out the
joyful prayer of the dawn from the minarets. The streets,
muddy and dirty, are deserted. The little markets and the
bazaars are still inhabited by the ghost cats of the night.
And the traveller does not know whether to direct his eyes
towards the illuminated, spacious architectures of the
Selimiye Mosque, or to the mysterious jig-saw of the covered
waggons, wicker baskets and boxes in the streets. The
mosque, which awakens while the full moon still reigns aloft,
and the sleeping market: the two faces of Orient, prayer and
the bazaar.

Two aspects of Zagreb, capital of
Croacia: The roofs of the St. Mark
church and embroidery works at the
market of Dolac.

But nobody responds to the muezzin who sings out from the high minarets of the Selimiye Mosque; nor to the muezzin who sings out from the battle-scared minarets of the Uscefreli Mosque; nor to the muezzin who sings out from the slender minarets of the Ula Mosque. Not even to the fountain flows in the spacious, square patio of the Kervansaray Hotel. The Turkish camel drivers no longer sleep with their turbulent sleep under its vaulted galleries. But the traveller, since it is night and the night belongs to whoever wants to inhabit it, dares to people the corners of Edirna with the characters of his imagination.
Ay, the sleeping markets! What mystery of tables and cats is there in the sleeping markets? There is a smell of ripe fruit and canvas, of leather slippers and wickerwork. Edirna is a market and a large mosque. But the traveller, when the full moon accompanies him along the deserted streets, cannot decide whether Edirna is more of a market or of a mosque.

The National Museum of Belgrade. Left, bottom, the Yugoslavian Parliament. Right: Shoeshop in Skopje, Macedonia.

Two views of Edirna, the first stop of the Orient Express in Turkey.

At daybreak, the grey pigeons flock the skies, with the clamour of broken clocks. Edirna is sky blue, like the rest of Turkey. Who painted Turkey with anil and skyblue? Turkey is the homeland of the nomads, the country of the men who paint their rooms with the skyblue colour of daybreak in the open air. Turkey is the country of the undulating roofs, of the houses which have never ceased to be a canvas tent blown by the wind in the middle of the way. The traveller breakfasts with the hot, dark early morning tea in a nameless tavern. The traveller, since he has nothing to dump in his glass of tea, accompanies his breakfast with a delightful Turkish cigar. The tavern's furnishing is old, noble and basic: three marble tables, a stove, a barrel with water used as a washbasin, a few solid wooden chairs and a calendar showing a dancing girl, a little fat for the taste of the period. An old man with a greying moustache and wrinkled face is warming his tea in his samovar. Some early rising peasants, seated around a table, savour the sweet cigarrette of the conversation. The smoke rises up the blue painted walls, forming baroque spirals, spirals which need not envy the dancing girl on the calendar.

The Orient Express traveller has seen Edirna by night. And be wouldn't like to see it by day now. As the doors of the markets of Edirna beging to open, slowly, afflictedly, the traveller shuts himself in his room at the Kervansaray Hotel and falls deeply asleep under the warmth of a ray of sun streaming in through the small window.

Sofia, the main stop of the Orient Express in Bulgary: one pope in front of the church of Svetka Petka, and one of the city parks.

Istambul: cemetery, eventide and end of journey

With the sea of Marmora to the right and the walls of
Byzantium to the left, the Orient Express runs into Istambul.
The day breaks clean and fresh and the traveller's eyes are
paintings spirals of air in the air, bubbles of water in the
water. Istambul is a ruin, a shipwreck of Europe on the banks
of Asia or a shipwreck of Asia on the banks of Europe.
While he strolls along the sad platforms of Sirkeci station,
the traveller thinks that Istambul is a ruin; but a ruin with a
soul, a failure of beauty in history, a shipwreck of intelligence
on the banks of the sea. Sirkeci is the last station in Europe,
the terminus of the West. Sirkeci is a station in ruins,

The monumental mosque of Ahmet in
Istambul, known as the Blue Mosque,
due to the blue shade of its tiles.

Flea market with Turskish souvenirs
and craftsmanship.

illuminated by broken windows, inhabited by the dust and by the clocks stopped with the resignation that goes nowhere. Through Sirkeci pass the men who, enmasked in their ashen faces, depart to look for fortune in Europe: with their baskets of fruit, with their torn suitcases, with their gold teeth.

The traveller climbs up along the steep narrow streets of old Istambul, mud and ruins, white minarets and leaden chimney smoke, to the hill of Eyüp, the highest place to where his legs carry him. Eyüp, city of miracles and of the dead, is the balcony of Istambul. It stands on the banks of the Golden Horn, overlooking a soft landscape of cypresses, mosques and ruined walls. The villas of Eyüp, where the high officials of the Turkish Empire lived, still have poetic names on their fallen doors: the Nightingale's Well, the Forty Cypresses, the Reservoir of Life, the Sea Bathe.

Eyüp was the district of flowers and water. Today it is the city of the dry fountain. The Turkish Empire is buried in its cemeteries.

The traveller is writing on a marble topped table, in front of a samovar in which the turbid tea of melancholy is steaming, in the same Café where Pierre Loti used to sit to listen to the tales of tramps. Pierre Loti was a sailor. The traveller prefers to tour the world in a third class carriage. And to discover, suddenly, when the sun sets behind the mosque of Eyüp that Istambul is coloured like a dove. But it smells of smoke. And of mutton. And of third class carriage.

The train finishes. And perhaps it sinks like Europe in the sea of Marmora. But the traveller, as he writes the full stop to the chronicle of his journey, on top of the hill of Eyüp, wonders whether the ruins also end up becoming smoke. The traveller prefers to think that ruin is immortality: an indelible memory of the man who travelled the world looking out through the window of a third class carriage.

Aspects of everyday life in Istambul:
the bear tamer, the shoeshiner, the
pidgeon food seller, and the fish seller
in front of the Galata Bridge.

The Publishers wish to acknowledge the
Wagons-Lits International Co, Madame
Ma. Teresa Bonnet, Monsieur Jean-Paul,
The Museum of Decorative Arts, and the
National Library of Paris for their valuable
assistance.

Printed in Spain  GEOCOLOR®

COGRAF,S.A. Dep. Leg. - B - 38.370 - 79